The Beautiful Book for

LOVERS

Laine Cunningham

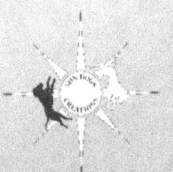

The Beautiful Book for Lovers

Published by Sun Dogs Creations
Changing the World One Book at a Time

Print ISBN: 9781946732736

Cover Design by Angel Leya

Copyright © 2018 and 2019 Laine Cunningham

All rights reserved. No part of this book may be reproduced in any form or by any means, electronic, mechanical, digital, photocopying or recording, except for the inclusion in a review, without permission in writing from the publisher.

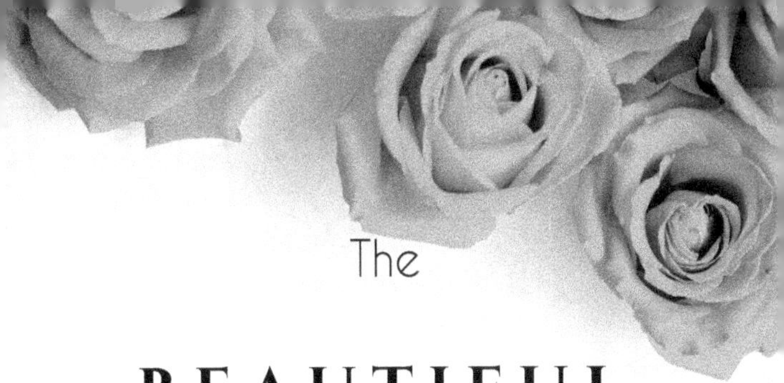

The

BEAUTIFUL

BOOK

SERIES

Align Your Passion With Your Purpose

Passion is a telegram addressed to the soul.

A joyful heart finds much to enjoy.

The soul's journey takes a lifetime.

Regret stirs a second chance.

Refresh your passion to reconnect with compassion.

Love is the best four-letter word.

You don't need to hold a hand to hold a heart.

A partner mirrors your truest self.

The ink written upon a heart never fades.

What you love reflects who you are.

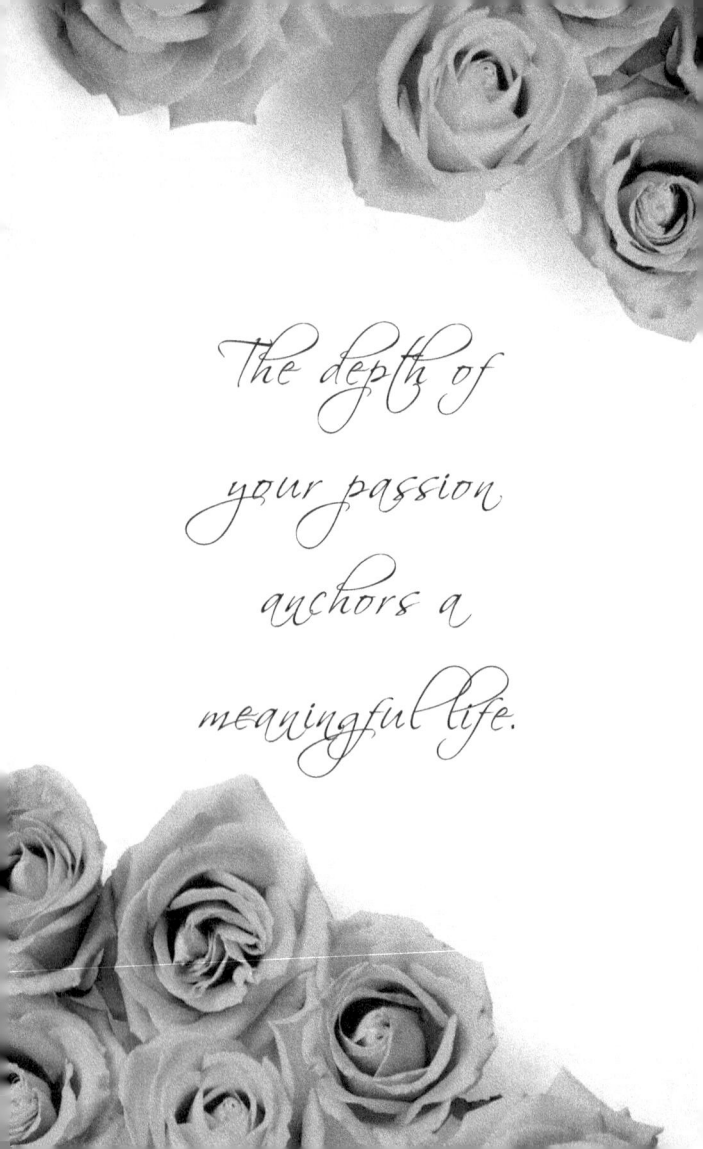

The depth of your passion anchors a meaningful life.

How you love tells the world how much you truly care.

Love has no

expiration date.

The world is as beautiful as the world within your heart.

Petals wither so that seeds can be sown.

When the heart sings,
the soul listens.

*When the soul leads,
the heart cannot break.*

A buttressed wall soars higher.

Even knights occasionally remove their armor.

The open hand can receive or give.

A tiny bit of sweet eliminates the sour.

Love yourself so that others can love you.

Touch everyone with your gentle nature.

The joy you share is the joy you inspire.

The strongest souls
are imbued with softness.

A note to a lover inscribes two hearts.

Ride the comet of love through the galaxy of your heart.

An expectant soul discovers electric love.

Love journeys through one past into multiple futures.

Love makes today lighter and tomorrow brighter.

Love that alights wants for nothing.

The tides of the heart will never fully recede.

Love's winter turns inward to build a deep connection.

All that is holy is housed within the heart.

The heart is to the head as the compass is to the map.

The longest journey explores the heart.

The lovestruck suffer

a delicious type

of pain.

The lyrics of love are composed anew every day.

Reciprocity balances the scales.

Dive into love and spread a wake of joy.

The unicorn

is captured by

the pure of heart.

Be as innocent in love
as the peaceful dove.

Love foresees the faded rose and continues to nurture the vine.

Love's value is weighed by the scales of the soul.

The heartbeat drives the tempo of love.

The pulse of your blood is the pulse of your passion.

The language
of love is

unique to each couple.

The light sparked by one couple illuminates many lives.

When two souls

form a couple,

each life is doubled.

The sacrament of love is the most sacred of all.

The heart is the foundry in which love is forged.

Love is a fever that needs no cure.

Love reveals that the horse is actually Pegasus.

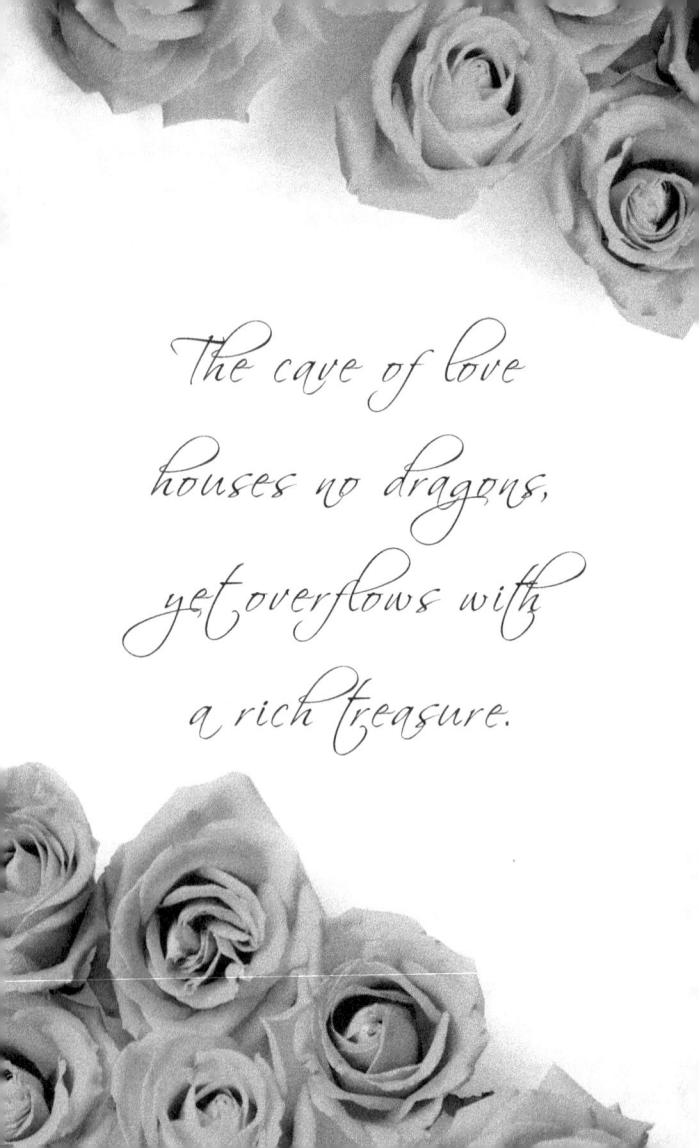

The cave of love houses no dragons, yet overflows with a rich treasure.

Love is an opera composed for two.

The richness of love ripens with desire.

When love awakes,
the planet tilts
in a new direction.

Beloved are those who are beloved to themselves.

The names of love are as varied as the lovers.

To be wooed

is to be invited

into your soul.

Love demands

no sacrifice,

although sacrifices

might be made.

Love makes no demands a lover is unwilling to provide.

Love is a truly unlimited resource.

*By daring to desire,
you also dare to dream.*

The most ardent lovers possess no hearts but their own.

The heart that would promise to another must first promise to itself.

When hunger leads to rapture, love's thirst grows more intense.

The strongest attachments form without constriction.

The appetite
of adoration
is gloriously craven.

Love is found at the intersection of hope and humility.

Love asks the soul

to rise higher.

The deepest love

plans for forever.

NOVELS BY LAINE CUNNINGHAM

The Family Made of Dust

Beloved

Reparation

OTHER BOOKS BY LAINE CUNNINGHAM

Woman Alone: A Six-Month Journey Through the Australian Outback

On the Wallaby Track

Seven Sisters: Spiritual Messages from Aboriginal Australia

Writing While Female or Black or Gay

The Zen of Travel
The Zen of Gardening
Zen in the Stable
The Zen of Chocolate
The Zen of Dogs

The Wisdom of Puppies
The Wisdom of Babies
The Wisdom of Weddings

The Beautiful Book of Questions
The Beautiful Book for Dream Seekers
The Beautiful Book for Rebels
The Beautiful Book for Women
The Beautiful Book for Lovers

Bikes of Berlin
Necropolises of New Orleans I & II
Ruins of Rome I & II
Ancients of Assisi I & II
Panoramas of Portugal
Nuances of New York
Glimpses of Germany
Impressions of Italy
Altitudes of the Alps
Knights Through the Ages
Coast of California
Utopia of the Unicorn
Flourishes of France
Portraits of Paris
Grandeur in the Republic of Georgia
Tableaus of Tbilisi

www.ingramcontent.com/pod-product-compliance
Lightning Source LLC
Chambersburg PA
CBHW071754080526
44588CB00013B/2233